In Their Shoes

(The Long Walk Away)

By Lana Lewis-Talib

Copyright Page:

For more information email authorlanat@yahoo.com

ISBN: 979-8-218-31159-9

A candid and intimate glimpse into the world of caring for someone suffering from dementia. Each chapter holds a memory and a lesson in the painful fight to love unconditionally and love beyond the changing faces of a loved one grappling to keep their old self alive.

Lana strikes a chord in opening her heart and putting into words her unfiltered thoughts and feelings while caring for her sister. A must-read for all, not just those who have family or friends with dementia but also those who are family or friends of many individuals who care for and love individuals in any stage of dementia.

Linky Ugeh, Editor & Author

No matter what the challenges, she always comes through with a solution. In this beautiful book the reader can see how many challenges she faced and how she tried to get over them. Lana is committed to her family, her community, and her religion. Highly recommend this book to EVERYONE. My dear Sister Lana: Much love and Prayers for you and your family, especially your sister.

Mussart Chaudhry, MD, Franciscan Health Network

This is a beautiful story of family, love, commitment, and suffering. Suffering, both as patient, family, friends, and caregiver. It's a gripping account of the deep love of a sister for her family.

It's a story of one's determination and how the family comes together at a challenging time. This book will make the reader cry. Many of us can relate to Lana's story from different angles: as patients, doctors, caregivers, siblings, or researchers. Lana has done a great job in this short memoir of her sister who is there but gone.

Doctor Halima Abdur-Rahman (Al-Khattba)

DEDICATION

This book is dedicated to my Mother Daisy Lewis. She personally taught me how to love, how to care for my siblings, and care for humanity overall. My Mother has passed away, but I believe if she were here, she would be my biggest cheerleader. Thank you for your love.

To my father Chester Lewis, the first person who ever told me "Your best friends are your sisters and brothers". He has passed away; however, I know that he was so proud of his children. Also, knowing my father as I did, he would love this book. Thank you for teaching me love.

Last but not least:

To Tiffany, my oldest daughter, thank you for always stepping up to support me with Connie.

To Tammy, Toyia and Yasmine, my daughters, thank you for your love and support.

To Yahya, my dear husband and loving supporter that has been there with me, step by step, never once disapproving of our lives being changed by moving Connie in with us and sharing in becoming her caregiver.

To my siblings for assisting when they could; you are appreciated.

FOREWORD ONE

As the daughter of the author, I find myself humbled and honored to introduce this touching story of my mother's journey through the complexity of dementia with her beloved sister. Prior to sharing my thoughts on the book, I want to share brief remarks about my aunt as I know and will always remember her.

Growing up, Aunt Connie was my favorite auntie. It wasn't because of what she could do for me, as typical for how kids measure an adult's love, but rather what felt like her commitment to connecting with me on my level. I remember times I would visit with my grandmother and Aunt Connie and they'd play games with us and ask questions about how we were doing beyond just school. I remember how SEEN and HEARD that made me feel. In honesty, it inspires the way I try to show up in my nieces' and nephews' lives. I know I won't always get it right but what Aunt Connie has taught me is that it's about showing up - how and when you can.

In the pages to come, you'll find a deeply personal story written by a sister, a caretaker - my mom. Sisterhood can be described in many ways but as Amy Li, is quoted as saying, "Having a sister is like having a best friend you can't get rid of. You know whatever you do, they'll still be there". And that's true of this story.

You'll read my mother's raw and unfiltered words as she describes her experience of watching my aunt gradually be impacted by dementia. When my mother embarked on this journey she had no roadmap, no guidebook, and no prior experience caring for someone with this type of dementia. Yet, through sheer determination and showing up for her sister as Aunt Connie had previously exhibited sisterhood, she did her best to offer love and patience.

You'll get to understand not only the life of my aunt Connie, who experiences dementia, but that of the author, the caregiver, and her perspective - challenges even. For those who have walked a similar path, this story will undoubtedly resonate and hopefully offer solace to those who may be faced with similar challenges.

We know dementia can take a relentless grip on the mind and dare I say soul, but its cruelty is underscored by this story. It robs individuals of their memories, identities, and ability to navigate the world they once knew. This disease like many others doesn't discriminate by age, wealth, or popularity. And in our case, it targeted my dear aunt, who had once been a vibrant and joyful soul.

This book is not just a chronicle of caregiving; it is a testament to the power of love and the resilience of the human spirit. Through tears, laughter, moments of confusion, and fleeting glimpses of recognition, an unwavering love for my aunt shines through. This book unveils the realness of our lives and bonds of family.

I hope that as you read on, you'll come to understand the complexities of dementia, but more importantly, that you recognize the enduring love that transcended the boundaries of memory loss - love transcends all.

May these pages serve as both a tribute to this herculean journey and a source of comfort to those who find themselves navigating the challenging waters of dementia alongside a loved one.

In love and transparency,

T. Leslie O'Rourke

T. Leslie O'Rourke

Vice President

Acquisition Marketing Strategy

FOREWORD TWO

I have known Lana Lewis-Talib for the last three decades. Throughout our many years of friendship, Lana has not only been a friend, but she has also been a sister to me that has displayed the true meaning of sisterhood through her character and actions. Her care and love for others encompasses all those around her, near and far. She always reaches out and extends her support to anyone going through hardships without hesitation. Lana has always had a passion for helping others by always supporting her family and serving her community.

In Their Shoes is a book that Lana wrote based on her sister's struggle with dementia. Dementia is an evil illness that causes a loved one, a person dear and close to the family, to become isolated from their family even when amongst them. It is sadly the loss of a loved one, even though they remain physically present. They become total strangers to you, more so, you to them.

As a human being it is normal to go into denial when such an atrocity strikes the family. It is always difficult to take the first step of taking on the very difficult task of addressing the situation head-on by seeking the needed and proper medical help.

Lana, of course, did not take the easy road and moved her sister in with her and was by her side every single day as her sister suffered from dementia. This book is full of emotions, and its details enlighten the reader with valuable tips and introduce them to the world of the dementia patient and those surrounding them. Lana has shared her very raw and very real experience with her sister, something that is not easy for anyone to share. Lana gives a real-life experience of the harsh realities of taking care of a dementia patient.

This book is not just an eye-opener for those taking care of a loved one with dementia, it provides support for anyone who is taking care of a loved one who is ill or going through tough times. It is always helpful to know that someone else has shared the same difficulties, fears, and concerns. That someone else has experienced the pain of seeing a loved one going through something so brutally awful.

Lana's sister's life will live on in support of others going through similar difficulties, thanks to her sharing her story.

Rana Al-Azm

School Principal
Houston Peace Academy

TABLE OF CONTENTS

INTRODUCTION

I am excited to usher you into the lives of several individuals who share several similarities. This work came about with me beginning to journal things that were taking place in my sister's life. My journaling began after her diagnosis, but I reached back to include some of who she was prior to her life sentence of this cruel disease called dementia.

As I continued to document events in my sister's life, I realized this had become a work that may benefit you as the reader with your friend or a loved one who may be experiencing early onset dementia. This will be helpful for whatever stage of the disease they may be in. Perhaps you'll find answers to some of your unanswered questions in this book as you navigate the journey with your loved one or friend.

I hope as you read each chapter you will begin to see a picture of what the walk is like in the shoes of those with dementia and those caring for them.

Having worked in the medical profession and my loving parents instilling love and compassion in me at an early age I thought for sure it offered me all I needed to take this on, hands down.

Boy was I wrong.

After some time had passed, I began to realize I needed as much care as I was giving.

There is a saying that goes "You can't pour from an empty vessel". It is extremely important to take the best care of yourself as possible. As you are giving you most certainly need to recharge. A few suggestions would be:

- Make a standing appointment for a manicure/pedicure.
- Include a massage on a regular basis.
- Taking time away, even short walks, to relax your mind can be beneficial.

It's not just an old cliche, *You can't give what you don't have*. For example, try paying a $50.00 gas bill with $20.00. What a stressful situation that would be!

I enjoy volunteering in the community I live in. I would encourage you to continue to participate in what interests you and stay active.

Grab a good book after you've put your loved one down for a nap, touch the pages as you read it may create the illusion of being away.

One of the best parts of myself care was when my husband and I took a vacation out of state. We enjoyed being together and away from caregiving if only for a week. Remember selfcare is equally as important as caregiving.

In this book you will find interesting real-life stories, research and resources that will provide you a helpful way to maneuver through the highs and lows of dementia/Alzheimer's.

PART 1: IN THEIR SHOES

CHAPTER 1: BEFORE THE DIAGNOSIS

There may be many of you who've had an experience with a loved one, friend, or someone who does not seem to be rational. This book may help you identify some early signs of dementia in your loved one.

I want to tell you who my sister Connie (Constance) was before her Dementia diagnosis. She was very loving and caring. She actually set her life aside to care for others, especially family members.

Connie and I are among thirteen siblings. My sister Connie was the third born, the second female in the family. She loved all her siblings and had a special love for all her nieces and nephews. They enjoyed being around her because oh, how she pampered them. She was the unspoken BIG MAMA of the family when it came to her siblings' children, though not to take the place of our mother, the TRUE GRANDMOTHER.

All my mother's grandchildren loved Connie, which included my own. Their faces would light up as she walked in the door. They would fight one another, pushing and shoving, to get to Connie first.

"Aunt Connie!" echoed down through the house as they were running to the door to greet her every time she would visit.

When it was time for her to go the air would feel thick with sadness. I'm telling you; you could even feel the thickness in the room when it was time for her to get ready to leave. Over and over, you would hear, "No, you can't stay all night with Aunt Connie this weekend." It was just such a treat to see how much love she had for them and they for her.

Connie has always been a nurturer. Shirley, our sister who was 2 years younger than Connie, married and moved to St. Louis, Missouri. After a few years in St. Louis, Missouri, Shirley became very ill. Shirley was suffering with multiple sclerosis (M.S.) causing her to lose her sight and became bedridden. Connie set her life aside and moved to St. Louis to care for her. Although Shirley's husband was still present, Connie cooked, cleaned and cared for her every need.

After a while, my sister regained her sight and even regained her strength. All Glory to the Most High for that miracle. After the death of her husband, Shirley was ready to move back to Indianapolis. That was perfect for all of us because we were all able to help care for her. After some time, my sister's health was on the decline again. Connie moved Shirley in with her and took very good care of her: from getting her signed up for Social Security Disability to bathing, feeding, and keeping her as active as she possibly could.

You might ask how Connie nurtured everyone. She was the best caregiver to anyone in our family that got sick. She literally set aside her needs or wants and whatever was going on in her life. I just love the way she helped. Connie felt that it was her duty to help nurse anyone in the family that was sick back to health. It was just natural for her. It was a given and she didn't seem to be bothered in any sense of the word, doing such duties for each and every person that needed it.

Similarly, Connie felt it was her duty to ensure that we looked our best. She could do this because she was a licensed cosmetologist. I recall her doing our hair and she made sure we looked especially good for the holidays! I can recall one time that I received a medical diagnosis and went to Connie, knocked on her door and when she opened the door, I fell into her arms and felt safe, comfortable and listened to by her. She rocked me, talked to me, comforted and assured me that God was going to make this alright.

I just began to feel so much better about the diagnosis I had gotten, and to this day I look back at that and think she opened her heart up, not just her arms, not just her door. Connie opened her heart and poured into me what I needed just to stand and know that it was going to be OK.

Now, she did have a mean streak in her, but we all knew that and worked hard to avoid that side of her. Connie's mean streak was one that I tried to avoid at all costs, but sometimes it found its way to me as well. She would be somewhat aggressive. She, by no means, was threatened by anyone. But as I explained, her mean streak was on the opposite end of the spectrum of her kind heart. She would do just about anything for you, but if you crossed her, it took her a long time to forgive.

As kind as my sister was to us, she must not have been as kind to her friends, because she would only have a friend for a short period of time and then the friendship abruptly ended. No one to laugh and chat with in person or on the phone.

Friendship wasn't something Connie had, so her world became a lot smaller. Her socialization was next to nothing. It was very difficult to see her not have friends as all her siblings have friends. We would extend invitations to her to join us on trips, birthday parties, family gatherings and so many other events that my sister missed because she simply would not go.

She did not want to participate in social activities much. Since she didn't have friends, she relied solely upon her family. Yes, we were there for her. Sometimes, however, she'd go shopping with us and remind us of how much she loved sweets. We'd shop at a few clothing stores then always end up having to go for some sweets. She loves peppermints and anything sweet for that matter.

In Connie's younger years she would take her three younger siblings to the State Fair each year. What a wonderful time we had. We would stay all day and still not be ready to go home when the fair was closing. Before she became distant, we could always count on seeing her. During the holidays she helped our mother with the Thanksgiving and Christmas dinner preparations. There was so much love and joy felt in our home all the time, especially during the holidays. As I reflect, I can almost smell the oyster dressing in the oven, the hot water cornbread on top of the stove, and the yams with the marshmallows on top. Not to mention the KYs that lit up the whole house! I can hear my mother saying to Connie, "You can go on and start the potato salad", which was Connie's specialty.

I can hear the laughter and joy that came from the kitchen with my sisters Connie, Shirley, and Gloria. I'm from the last set of children born to Mama and Daddy. Deborah, Linda and I (the last 3) would be playing with gifts sitting on the stairs trying to hear what they were saying and doing. Then the doorbell would ring, and it would be two of our other sisters, Annette and Delores (Cookie) laughing and cracking jokes as they entered the house. Oh, just sitting here, thinking back brings tears to my eyes and a huge smile to my face.

Something else that brings tears to my eyes is the lack of pictures of Connie's younger years. For some reason, Connie never liked seeing herself captured in print. She would routinely tear up photos of herself. You might think it's because Connie didn't like her appearance but that wouldn't explain the reason that she even destroyed her baby photos and elementary school pictures. In fact, I was only able to locate one picture of her wedding day!

Connie's wedding picture.

Connie and I some years after she got married.

Connie and my granddaughter, A'miya, a year before Connie moved in with me.

Connie helping at the Homeless Shelter.

Connie frying green tomatoes.

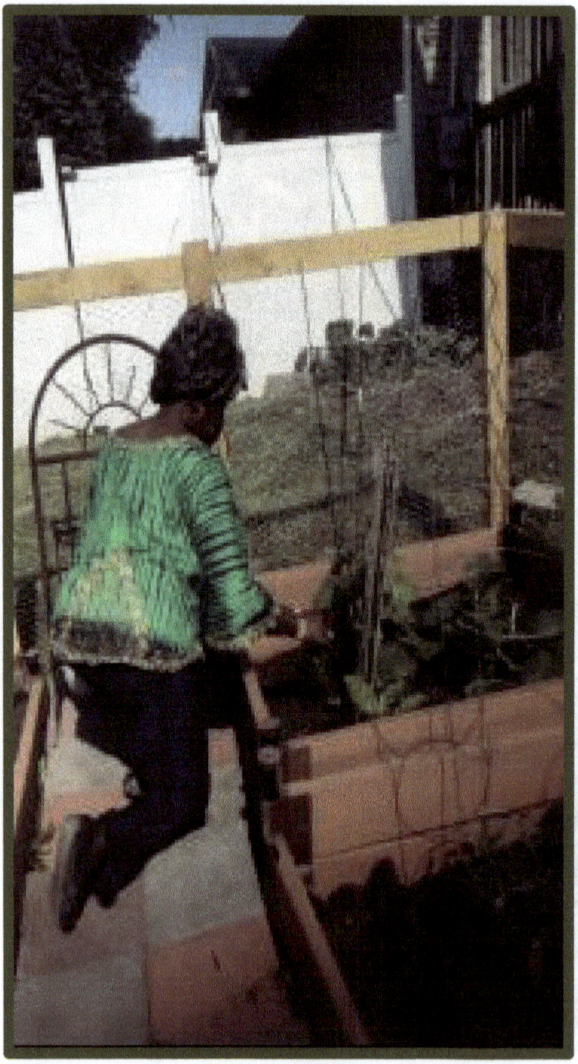

Connie collecting tomatoes from the garden.

One of the pictures of Connie in her younger days.

Connie's Potato Salad recipe

Ingredients:

1 dozen eggs
5 pounds potatoes
Chopped celery
1 bell pepper, chopped
Mustard
Vinegar
Mayonnaise
Sugar
Paprika
Salt and Pepper

Directions:

1. In a large pot, boil the eggs and potatoes. Boil until the potatoes are soft.

2. Chop celery and peppers.

3. Smash most of the potatoes and cube the rest.

4. Chop the eggs into small pieces. Save two to three eggs to slice to add to the top of the potato salad.

5. In a large bowl, mix all the ingredients to desired consistency.

6. Add vinegar, salt and pepper to taste.

7. Top with sliced eggs and paprika.

Note: I can't share the exact amounts because that's Connie's secret.

Chapter 1 - Reflection Questions

1) What was your initial thought after hearing of your loved one's diagnosis?

2) What was he/ she like before the diagnosis?

CHAPTER 2: THE START

When Connie was in her mid-30s, she married a very nice man, Gene Autry Clark, who loved her and her entire family so much. We loved him to pieces. Connie had such a wonderful relationship with her husband. Their marriage was to me a model marriage that I could look at as a goal for my own marriage. From Connie's marriage, as a child, I learned what I wanted for my married life.

Connie and Gene had that type of marriage that anyone would envy. They did things together that made me look at them with admiration. I couldn't wait until I reached the age of marriage. I looked forward to sharing my life with somebody the way they shared their lives together. Her husband was such a genuine man. The love that the two of them had for one another was impeccable. It was very devastating for Connie to lose the love of her life and for them not to have produced any children from that marriage, which devastated her even more.

Connie and Gene always believed that there would be time later to start their family. Gene became ill one day while at work. Connie insisted that he allow her to take him to the hospital; he never returned home. He developed an aneurysm and passed away after a short stay in the hospital's intensive care unit.

After the death of Connie's husband, there was a big change in her personality. Her mean streak became more intense, and the frequency increased. It seemed that she began to isolate herself from everyone and stopped going on outings, cookouts and gatherings. It seemed we weren't important to her anymore. I can't recall her crying much but she seemed so sad most of the time. She removed all the pictures of her husband from the wall and the small frame pictures that she had had around her house. I would guess it was simply too hard for her to look at knowing she would not see him anymore. Once her husband's life insurance policy paid out the beneficiary's payment, she bought a house, and I moved in with her. I recall Connie dating a few different times, but I don't remember much to even mention of anyone after the loss of her true love, her husband, Gene.

Something that didn't change about her was her ability and excitement about beautifying her living space. She always did her own decorating, but you would have sworn she hired a consultant or decorating company because that's how great it always was. Connie's home interior decorating skills are something that always amazed me no matter where she lived. Connie had wonderful taste in household items and furnishings. Her place, whether a house or apartment, always looked fabulous. She had the best of everything: the furniture, the carpet, the curtains. I remember in one apartment everything in the living room was black and white leather, the sofa loveseat and the chaise. I think at that apartment she had accented the decor with a little red. It was just so awesome when you walked in and she always had a wonderful oil burning so it smelt amazing as well. I'm sure she got that great gift of decorating from our mother.

It was at this time that Connie began to exhibit behaviors that were not normal for the average person. She would move from one location to another. When she lived on the northwest end of Indianapolis in a very nice apartment for residents 'over 55', she began to tell us siblings stories of people doing things to her. For example, neighbors beating on her walls, entering her apartment, or tampering with food in her refrigerator. She spoke of a handicapped senior citizen neighbor who had inappropriate relationships with men in the building. We suspected these things could not be happening. At this point, Connie had moved to another location in the city, and the stories became even more unbelievable and bizarre. She was still going to the grocery store, visiting family, enjoying her life, but from time to time we would hear outrageous stories from her. We began to wonder how likely it was that these things could be happening. I recall one time Connie asked me to come to her apartment to go to her office with her because the office staff was saying things out of line to her and being very rude. I wasn't sure about this because maybe she had upset them for some reason, but I decided to go with her. I recall a woman in the office being very kind to her, no ill will, no rudeness.

As we left the office, Connie said, "I should take you every time. She was nice because you were with me; now that she knows I can call my sister, she will probably be nice from now on".

By now I knew something wasn't right. I began to pay closer attention to her and the things she would tell us. I wanted what Connie said to us to be reality because I didn't want anything to be wrong with her, but that was not the case.

Soon she wanted to move out to another apartment. When we moved her, it was the third time in three years, again to another senior living location. We all agreed that after Connie decorated it, it could have been a picture from a magazine. It wasn't long before she began to have difficulties with this management, and she felt it was no longer a safe place for her. She told us that the manager and his wife were doing things to her such as raising her rent, coming in and tampering with her food while she was away, or speaking rudely to her. All these things we'd heard before about other management teams. It was time to move again.

With all these moves, inevitably it would not be long before her beautiful furniture would be destroyed by family because they were not professional movers. Moving had become very difficult for the sisters and me. The brothers had gotten older and were unable to move heavy furniture.

Connie's behavior became more outlandish as time passed. She told us people were following her.

"I saw one of them in the store and he just kept looking at me. I wanted to go back to the store and ask for help, but I just walked home. He kept following me even as I walked." We started picking her up to take her places she needed to go, but even when we were with her, she would say things like "There's one of them – the guys that keep following me".

She would say to me, "Look, you see him."

I saw people in the store, but no one was looking at her. Connie got so angry if you didn't agree with her. I would say things like "Well, let him look. He can't take both of us down" to keep her from getting angry, not knowing exactly how to deal with it.

We moved Connie yet again to another apartment still on the west side of town. With that move, she lived closer to me, so I was the sibling who would check in on her most often, though all the siblings helped. One day I received a frantic call from Connie, screaming and crying, saying come and help me. All I could think was my worst nightmare had come true – she had done something to someone, and they had hurt her. She said this man was jumping on her. Driving to her home as fast as I could, calling my siblings from the car, I put out a family APB and we all raced to her apartment. When we arrived, Connie was in her apartment crying, telling us that a man had hit her in the stomach. I went to the apartment she was pointing to; I was so angry that I don't remember what I said at his door. One of my siblings called the police who investigated. The way Connie described the incident, it was *not* possible that it could have happened. The elderly man down the hall said no such thing happened. No one in the building heard or saw anything. The police asked if she had dementia. We answered NO SHE DOES NOT!

But, about that time we all began to realize these things were a figment of her imagination. When a year had passed at this apartment and Connie decided to move again, she moved into an apartment that was not only for senior living, and it was two blocks from my home. I felt this might be better because I could check in on her more often and go places with her. I contacted a mover to move her belongings. This apartment, like all of them she lived in, was very nice. She lived there for about a year and a half while she got progressively worse.

For instance, she claimed the utility wires outside her front room window were making her lights go on and off and causing her light bill to be extremely high. She said people were looking in on her from those wires. All I could think was OMG, not already PLEASE! I tried to comfort her by telling her to keep the blinds closed and just not to go to the windows. One day when visiting her, I noticed that she had taken the mattress off her bed and placed it in front of her bedroom window.

When I asked her, "What is going on?!"

Connie responded, "I don't want them looking at me in my bed."

I replied "Okay." I was drained.

As usual, as time passed, problems began to arise with the neighbors and management. When maintenance came into her apartment, she began to hide things so they would not steal them. But now she couldn't find them when she needed them, like her keys, cell phone, or her wallet.

My sister Linda had given Connie two very nice chairs that once belonged to our mother. They were of such great quality from when furniture was sturdy and made of real wood. They were passed down to Linda from our mom before she died. Connie, being the oldest sister, Linda had passed them to her. One day, pulling up to Connie's apartment and seeing the chairs in the parking lot almost took my breath away. I couldn't wait to get up to her apartment, so I called her as I drove in.

"Connie, what are the chairs doing out here on this lot?"

Her response, in a calm voice, "I threw them over the balcony because I couldn't carry them down the stairs. I'm going to throw them away. I should never have let Linda give me these raggedy chairs."

I was so upset with her that I immediately called Linda, but there was nothing much we could do. They were now destroyed. I didn't help her drag them across the lot to the dumpster. I didn't have a good visit that day.

We all confirmed with Connie that she lived on the top floor in this building. She would still tell us people were beating on the floor, making loud noises, and disturbing her at night. The neighbor across the hall and Connie were initially very friendly. She began to have problems with her as well. She was a very old lady, and we realized Connie was going to cause this senior lady's family to become very irritated with her. My fear was that they would do something to Connie. We did all we could to keep Connie from causing problems with anyone, but most of all with senior citizens because the repercussions for messing with someone's elders could turn out bad.

My sisters and I would plead with Connie to go to the doctor. We wanted to understand what was going on with her, but she refused every time we asked. Once when she agreed to let me go with her to a routine doctor's exam, I was so excited I called my sisters to let them know! My stomach was so nervous, anticipating talking to Connie's doctor and telling her what I thought was going on with Connie, I almost backed out of even opening my mouth about it but I knew we needed to get some answers, so I spoke up and told her what I thought. When the doctor finished her exam and asked if we had any questions I quickly spoke up and said Connie was displaying some early signs of dementia. I had worked with some dementia patients so I thought that might be what was going on. The doctor agreed to do an assessment. Connie was referred to a dementia specialist at a clinic called 'Healthy Aging Brain'.

The look that Connie gave me let me know that she was not happy with me. However, I couldn't take it back and I knew I needed to say the things I said in order to get the help for Connie that I felt she needed. She rolled her eyes at me and shifted her body to one side to block me out of her sight. That's how mad she seemed to be with me. I recall we had been seated in one of the patient's rooms, closest to the nurse station, it was a rather small room. It was extremely uncomfortable for me; sitting in silence with Connie refusing to acknowledge my presence. I wished the doctor had left the door open. Basically, I was just happy to hear that Connie had dementia instead of something else. When I returned home from that appointment, I shared that a diagnosis had been made and she had a follow-up appointment. I thought it would be good if we could all go with Connie.

Connie at a Christmas gathering with some of my mother's grandchildren.

Chapter 2 - Reflection Questions

1) Do you recall any tragedy in their life that may have occurred?

2) From your perspective, what was the impact of the tragedy?

CHAPTER 3: WATCHING THE DOORS CLOSE

Connie has now moved into my home with my husband and I. This phase of her dementia is very heartbreaking. I began to see a woman who I no longer recognized as being my sister. She even looks a little different. She looks broken. This part of this vicious disease appears to be so hard on a person.

Now, Connie is at home with me every day, though she does spend a little time with other family members a few days out of each month. I try to keep her active with reading, writing, watching TV, and doing as many different activities as her mental capacity allows.

She has begun to ask, “Do you think you can take me home?”.

This is after she has lived here for over four years. Some days she doesn’t realize that this is her home. She asks questions like “What time does the last bus run so I can catch it and go home?” Connie even thinks that her home is our old family home that she hasn’t lived in for over 30 years. In fact, no family member has lived there for ten years. When asked where she lives, she gives our old family address. It is so devastating to watch someone you love go through this. In addition, she began asking about deceased family members. Connie wants to visit or call them, even asking how our mother is doing. She becomes very emotional when I remind her that our mother is deceased. This too is hard on me having to relive and discuss the death of our mother and watch Connie become emotional.

It seems to me a daunting task for Connie to properly dress herself anymore, so this is another task I must assume. I get the clothes out for Connie to dress herself. At times, she would look at them and look so puzzled and confused as to what she should do with the top that I had chosen for her. I would hand her the top and she would just take it and move it to the other side of the bed.

I tell her, "Connie, please put your top on!"

Connie did not have a clue as to what I wanted her to do. She was just moving it around and then put it on the dresser and she just didn't understand the concept of dressing herself anymore. That for me was very difficult as it was something that it seemed she lost the ability to do overnight. This again was hard for me. I now know, as I say, I have that as another chore for myself to do.

I'll be honest, I did not sign up for this. As Forrest Gump would say, "Life is like a box of chocolates, you never know what you're gonna get."

I had no idea just how much moving Connie in with me would change ***my*** family life, but I would have it no other way. Sometimes people think of long-term care facilities for those seniors who are unable to care for themselves. I understand that may be best for some people, yet it has never been something our family believed in. At the end of the day, Connie has a home here with me as long as I'm here, if that is the will of God.

Sometimes I sit and talk with my sister, but she seems to be losing her ability to articulate.

Most days she will begin a conversation, then say, "That's ok, I don't know what I'm saying."

Sometimes her words are not clear or even sensible. I can see she is struggling to do what most people easily do to have a normal conversation. This is so heartbreaking.

I enrolled Connie in an adult senior day service center where she was able to participate in crafts, socialization, physical and mental activities, things people of her own age were doing. I visited several centers before making the decision on which location. The center was close to my home. The staff seemed very kind and professional. There was a daycare on the other end of the building. The administration shared with me that the interaction of toddlers and seniors is so uplifting for both groups. Each week the toddlers were allowed to visit the seniors with supervision.

This center had a licensed physical therapist on staff who worked with the seniors on an 'as needed' basis with prior consent from a family member or POA. This was a plus, as Connie had been diagnosed with arthritis, so she could benefit from the treatments as she needed it. She attended Monday through Friday from 8:00-4:30. The center provided breakfast, lunch, and a light snack, as well as transportation to and from the center. Connie seemed to enjoy this, until we were hit by the worldwide pandemic.

Connie's safety is very important to me, so I needed to remove her from the adult service center. There were just not enough staff in attendance to keep all the seniors safe. Most of the people at the adult day service were no longer able to do self-care such as washing their hands after they go to the bathroom or keeping their food on their own tray. Those with dementia do not have the discernment to not pick up things off the tables that may or may not have been sanitized well enough. It boiled down to the fact that there just were not enough staff members to give me that level of comfort that Connie would be safe in their care after the COVID pandemic started.

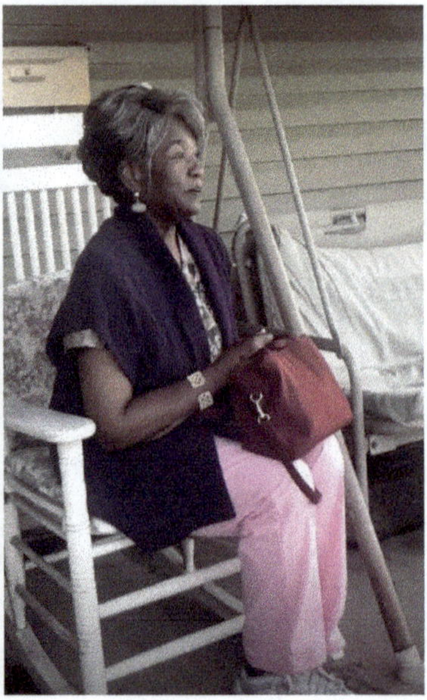

Connie on her way to Adult Day Service. In the days when she could still dress herself, still loved her makeup and doing her hair.

Connie in a rickshaw at the day service

Chapter 3 - Reflection Questions

1) Do you recall when you felt it was time for more help?

2) What are your thoughts on Adult Day Service Centers for seniors?

CHAPTER 4: CONNIE'S EGYPT TRIP

Long before Connie began to exhibit strange behavior, she began sending money monthly to sponsor an African child. She always talked about taking a trip to Africa, so when two of my sisters decided to go to Egypt, yes, Connie decided to go with them. My siblings tell me this trip was so refreshing just to see how much joy it brought to Connie. She talked about this for years. She never really talked about going anywhere else, so this trip was monumental for her. We are all grateful she was able to take this trip. She was indeed lucid enough to enjoy the trip, and they took lots of pictures which they put into a book to remind her of the trip.

The trip had a huge impact on Connie. She talked to me about the trip for weeks after she returned home. When Connie and I would look at the book from her trip to Egypt, she would light up and have so much joy in telling me, "Oh, I remember when I put my hands in the water in the Nile River, my hands felt so good just splashing around lightly in the water".

It was such a beautiful feeling for me hearing Connie sharing her stories. Connie went on to say that she had ridden a camel, saw the Pyramids, and so much more. It seemed as if her dementia was gone. I so enjoyed listening to her relive the many stories she had to share from her trip. I loved hearing the stories so much I wish I had gone with her, but watching her face as she shared with me was so delightful and more than made up for my not going along. I remember thinking, '(My how wonderful! I'm so happy she had the opportunity to do this'.) Then her story changed.

She said, "You know I was a little afraid to ride on the camel, so I chose to just kind of lay back and not do that. Instead, I watched Linda and Gloria as they rode the camels and wished I could have got my nerve up to hop on that camel!".

"It's OK you did what you wanted to do and I'm just so happy and overjoyed that you were able to do it."

I hoped she could stay on this side of her dementia, but a few weeks was all it lasted. I was excited and ran to get the book and sat down beside her as she had just finished her lunch and I would say to her, "Let's go through your book!" The book of pictures from her Africa trip was all I had to help her recall the experience.

I turned to the first page and asked, "Where were you there?"

Connie replied, "That's not me! Who is that?"

I thought, 'Oh boy, could this be true?! She doesn't know who this is.' So, I turned to another page, and I asked, "Who is this?".

She said, "Oh, I don't know. She looks a little like me".

I thought of all the joy we had of looking at this book and feeling like she was almost back to who she used to be. It was all gone just that quickly. My heart just sank. I was devastated because I then knew the few short weeks of her being on this side of her dementia were over. I had to remove myself from the room and go into my bathroom and cry. I thought we were headed back in the other direction but no, dementia decided it wanted to slide back in and continue this decline. This is painful, but I will never give up showing her the book in hopes that somewhere within her she gets some joy looking back on her once-in-a-lifetime trip.

Chapter 4 - Reflection Questions

1) Are you taking time to process your emotions?

REMEMBER: Breathe and tell yourself it's okay.

CHAPTER 5: THE TRIAL OF CAREGIVERS

Connie's first caregiver, Tonya, was as sweet as could be. She felt like a daughter to me. Tonya took great care of Connie, and she was prompt, professional, and courteous. She seemed to enjoy her job and being able to care for Connie. Tonya was a big help to us in bathing Connie, getting her meals, and interacting with her. Tonya wasn't one for asking a lot of questions as it pertained to her responsibilities to Connie. After she had been given her first instructions on her first day, she seemed to know how to carry that all through. Unfortunately, for us, but great for her, she returned to school to finish her degree, so she was unable to stay on as Connie's caregiver.

Now, with the second caregiver, Betty, there was a world of difference. She was also a very kind lady, but she was 75 years old. Betty was truly not capable of doing most of the tasks of the position. She had some limitations. For example, Betty used a walking cane. She had gout which caused lots of pain and further limited her mobility. Due to this, Betty didn't have the physical stamina to bathe Connie or take Connie out for a walk. Unfortunately, I made the mistake of allowing her to stay because I felt sorry for her. I moved my needs aside and placed hers upfront. I felt like she needed the money, or she wouldn't be working but at the same time, I needed the care for my sister. For two weeks I allowed her to come out of pity, but then I had to think about what it was doing, and it was unfair to myself and to Connie.

The goal was to make sure I was getting the best care for Connie as possible. I had to let her know that it was no longer possible for me to allow her to come because I didn't think she was meeting the needs of my sister, which was an extremely difficult conversation for me. It took me a few weeks, even months before I even allowed anyone else to come because I was so sad about how I had to let the last caregiver go.

Moving on to the third caregiver, she was a younger caregiver, like the first, knew her job, did it well, and she seemed to genuinely care about Connie. But my goodness, she lacked work ethic. She became very comfortable at our home. However, after a few weeks, her attendance became a problem. She was late at least 3 days a week and called off one day a week. It wasn't as if I had something to do every day, but sometimes I needed a break, if nothing more than to lie and rest for the four hours the caregiver was scheduled. It was such a relief for me when she came, so when she didn't and this was getting too often, I realized I needed to let her go.

Then, to make matters even worse, it got to the point where she even wanted to start bringing her child with her! These behaviors were totally unacceptable. Once again, we were without a caregiver because I had to let the agency know that I no longer wanted the service from her.

When I called to let the agency know that the young lady had called in yet again and wouldn't be at our home giving care that day, they never found a replacement. This was sometimes the hardest thing for me because I had already scheduled my own doctors or dental appointments. I just wanted to know that I had that day off to do what I needed to do; I was very unhappy with not just the young lady but the agency themselves. It's hard when you are looking forward to having help, but the help never arrives. It turns out that this young lady was a family member of the owner of this agency, so I didn't think we could get proper staffing.

My next step was to try once again to find professional and dependable help at the house with Connie. We moved to another company for services.

Connie had a new caregiver, Stacy; she felt more like family to us. She knew her job and she did it very well. Stacy was very consistent and patient, both attributes are extremely helpful! For Connie, consistency and patience help her have a regular routine and it seems to give her a slight sense of independence. I think Connie feels that consistency offers her what she needs at this point in her life. Such as knowing to put her own shoes on means she will be going for a walk, and sitting in a certain spot in the room means she will be working on her coloring sheets. Yet when she's in another chair that indicates to her that it's lunch time. These are just a few examples of how it seems to be helpful for Connie. Stacy had a routine that she followed every day with Connie. She kept Connie active. It's so important for Connie to be mentally and physically active. Connie needs to continue to do as much as she can to try to keep her disease as much at bay as possible. Physical activity is equally important if Connie stops moving then the brain will tell her she is incapable of moving. She can become bedridden, and that opens another door for many other problems medically, physically, as well as psychologically.

Stacy took her out walking as part of the physical activity. In addition, she worked with her on coloring on the sheets and workbooks that I provided for her. She did exercises like range of motion, talked to her, and kept her engaged. One of her previous caregivers, *when she would show up*, must have believed that it was her job just to come and be a companion i.e. sit and watch TV with Connie. I always found myself asking her to do things with Connie, and that got old fast! Stacy allowed me time to get out and take care of things that I need to take care of including taking care of my mental well-being. I was extremely comfortable and confident that when I stepped away, Connie was receiving the care that I expected for her.

Before this caregiver it was so difficult for me. Some of the others did such a disservice to my sister and most nights I was unable to sleep thinking about all the things that I needed to get done because I had to spend most of the previous day watching the caregiver as she was watching Connie! They were unable to properly offer the services that they were being paid to do. This caused me such anxiety, and as you may imagine, it began to really bother me that Connie was no longer able to take care of herself without the help of a caregiver. A caregiver is necessary to allow me to do the things that I need to do like handling my own affairs. I was pleased to have this new caregiver and it seemed as though Connie was as well. Stacy was with us for one year and realized that she had to move to another position to make more money, a living wage.

So once again, I had to find another caregiver and build my trust before I felt comfortable leaving Connie alone with them and feel confident that she was receiving an adequate level of care. Finding and keeping a reliable caregiver is more difficult than caring for the family member with dementia. I have come to realize that hourly compensation for this type of work is not sufficient compensation; it's not an easy job and requires more skills than people realize. It's neither a glamorous nor easy position.

Chapter 5 - Reflection Questions

1) Have you thought about how adding someone else to this dynamic would have an effect, good or bad?

2) Have you considered how important it is to do extensive interviews to ensure the best possible outcomes?

CHAPTER 6: REFUSING HOSPICE

Connie is losing an alarming amount of weight now. It's at this place that I'm told by her nurse practitioner (NP) to give her whatever she wants – sweets, snacks, anything to help maintain her weight. I fear the dementia has affected her brain's ability to maintain a healthy weight. It was very concerning to me that the NP repeated the same thing – "give her whatever she wants". That's not what I wanted to hear. I wanted a pill, some drops, or a medicine to help her with her weight, but her NP didn't seem to think there was anything they could do as it related to her weight loss.

Connie still sees herself as that large lady who used to weigh 150 pounds or even 185 at times. It's been years since she weighed anything over 130 pounds. When she's given a compliment – "you look good" – she reverts to her heaviest weight in her brain and rejects the compliment saying, "not me with my fat self".

One day, I was shocked and dismayed by what I heard at Connie's appointment. Connie's nurse practitioner (NP) said, "In my professional opinion, the time has come to place Connie in hospice."

Connie's nurse practitioner had staged Connie in the final stages of dementia based on things that were going on in Connie's life: the weight loss, the inability to have conversation, to articulate, put words together, to be able to feed herself are the things that she told me would be found in the later stages of dementia.

Now let me tell you, that struck a nerve with me. As she continued to talk and make this seem to be such a wonderful idea, I began to close out any thoughts of it. I had to replay that in my head. HOSPICE – did I hear her right? I didn't see Connie being at that stage, and I struggled thinking of placing her in hospice while living with me, or some other place, just waiting to die. Connie had stopped eating and had begun to lose a lot of weight, but I didn't see myself enrolling her in hospice. So, I refused and continued to care for her.

Placing Connie in hospice was never an option for several reasons. It's just something that the family I grew up in never considered with any of our loved ones. I worked at a few facilities, and I saw how the seniors were treated or mistreated is the proper word. The idea of knowing that it's possible that she may not get her meals on time if at all. Connie may be allowed to sit in her own urine for only God knows how long or even worse, her own feces. At some facilities that I have visited, you walk in and even smell the level of care or should I say the lack of care. I was not going to allow that for my sister. As long as God allowed me to care for her, I would care for her in my home.

When I started offering her pureed food, she began to eat all her food. Some days I still had to feed her, but she would finish it all. I would sometimes find myself saying over and over, "Come on Connie, eat some more, come on".

I quickly learned that sometimes trying to redirect Connie took longer than just doing it myself!!

At Connie's next appointment with her NP, I was able to share the changes that had been made. Oh, I was so happy to show her how Connie had begun to put back on a little weight and was a bit steadier on her feet. This is how things will go for my sister for now anyway. I know there is no turning this disease around or even slowing it down. It's my plan to do the best I can for Connie and know she'd do the same for me.

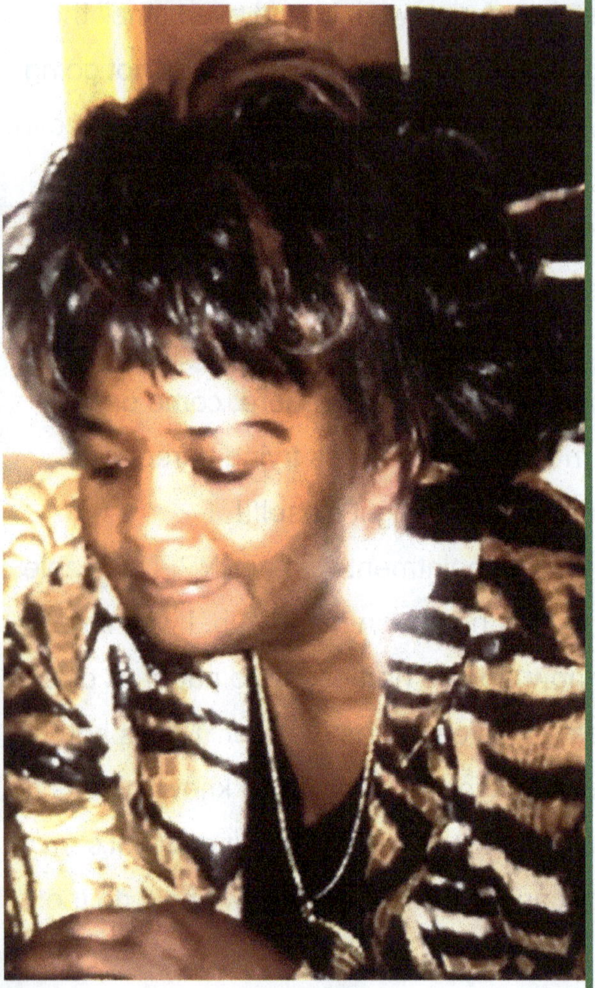

Connie at her heaviest weight.

Chapter 6 - Reflection Questions

1) Do you realize you are now making decisions about someone else's life?

2) Do you know it's perfectly fine to be an advocate for your loved one?

3) Do you know you don't have to always agree with the decision of the medical profession?

Have a POA on file.

CHAPTER 7: NO WAY OUT

This terminal illness seems to be moving into its final stage. When most terminal illnesses reach a certain point, you can begin to see the days becoming shorter for your loved one. It's hard for us to put a time on anyone's life expectancy, although with the miracle of modern science, you start to see things that show you things could very well be drawing near an end. Some of the things I see with Connie's illness truly sadden me.

I am so grateful to have her with me and even more grateful for the humor that sometimes comes with disease. Connie does some things that are so humorous. I would never laugh at my sister or her illness, but sometimes she'll say something that I find extremely funny. You will find, if you have been around someone with dementia or Alzheimer's, this is something that I think is just an added piece to give caregivers a bit of ease during this hardship.

At this point, some individuals with dementia will begin to use wheelchairs because they no longer are capable of walking. Some may have feeding tubes for when the brain doesn't understand how to swallow anymore.

I've had to alarm doors to make sure I'm alerted when the front or back doors are opened. I had a bed alarm put on Connie's bed so I would know when she got up during the night. Another piece of helpful equipment is the powered bath chair, which saved my back. It can be raised and lowered with a remote control. We bought an alert necklace so that in the event she got out of the house it would alert us to her location. That piece of equipment didn't last long after she took it off in the house and lost it. Once I found it, I discontinued the service. It would be of no use to us.

I used to let Connie sit on the front porch alone from time to time. Now she is no longer able to sit alone because she may wander off the porch. In the backyard, we have a koi pond with 30 plus fish and I don't trust that Connie would be safe alone out there either.

We have a vegetable garden that Connie helped me put out and tended the first year she was with me. We had so much fun planting and watching everything grow. Our first year of gardening together we picked things from the garden for salad. We fried green tomatoes, ate okra, green beans, and collard greens. We even had a watermelon! At one point she could be trusted to go out by herself to the garden and harvest some of the vegetables. Now she can't be left alone outside. I really do struggle just missing the sister that is gone, yet here.

I want to get back to talking about how this disease is so unpredictable. Connie was on a pureed diet for some time. The company that delivered meals had a glitch in their system so some of the customers were unable to receive their meals. I then began to purchase her meals from the local grocery, and they were not the pureed meals that she had been accustomed to.

It was so surprising to me when Connie's caregiver shared with me that she didn't have to tell Connie to finish her food. Connie was eating it all by herself. Connie used to play with the pureed food and just stir it around and wouldn't eat, so much that the caregiver and I began to feed her or assist in helping her finish it. She was put on those pureed meals at my request because she seemed to no longer be able to swallow regular food. She was just holding most of her food in her mouth. This was the cause of some of the weight loss that I mentioned previously.

I sometimes watch Connie as she interacts with her caregiver. I asked myself is it possible that Connie knows what she's doing? She will do things with the caregiver that she knows are not acceptable when I'm around.

If I'm looking from a distance, I see these things. Yet when I walk in the room, she stops as if she was never doing anything. I simply find it hard to understand how this disease impacts the brain that way. As I said earlier, Connie and most people with this disease, somehow have the ability to mask what's going on.

It was not until she moved in with me and even then, it took a while for me to see that her brain was reacting and acting to things very differently from the norm. I guess you might be wondering, "like what?". One example is she would jump up out of the chair and tell the caregiver, "You don't tell me what to do!"

"I'm going home!"

If I walk in the room, she sits down and I'll ask her, "Where are you going?".

She would say, "Oh nowhere, we're just sitting here".

My question is to myself, could this be because she doesn't know the caregiver as well as she knows me?

"Or is she truly capable of manipulating the caregiver?"

Is it even possible that that could be what's going on here?!

I watched Connie one day as she became a bit agitated and aggressive with the caregiver over her water bottle. I stepped back to see how long this would go on and if the caregiver knew how to take control of the situation to ensure that neither one of them would get hurt. Finally, I walked in the room and told Connie" Release the water bottle. The caregiver knows what she's doing," I reassured her.

"Connie, please don't treat her this way if you can help it".

Connie responded, "Okay".

I began to wonder if we were entering into the phase of her dementia that her doctor had asked me about from time to time. The questions go something like this:

"So has she become aggressive with you?"

"Does she use language that is inappropriate?"

"Is she refusing care?"

My answers until now are, “Absolutely not!”

Now I am paying closer attention to these behaviors to keep track of them, I am now aware that this new phase of her dementia has moved in and begun to unpack its unpleasant baggage.

Chapter 7 - Reflection Questions

1) Have your expectations on the impact of the diagnosis become a reality?

2) What would you do differently?

CHAPTER 8: A TYPICAL DAY

A typical day for Connie and I when she first moved in with me was quite different from today.

Connie and I would get up in the mornings and make breakfast together, laughing and talking. In the warmer months we would sit out on the porch and watch the birds and just listen to the peaceful sound of the crickets and the birds. She would help me with things around the house like washing dishes, folding and putting away laundry. I had to stop Connie from doing the dishes. I noticed a few times that there were still food particles on the dishes that she had put away into the cabinets. Shortly after, I realized that maybe that was no longer something I would rely on her to do. It wasn't easy because she continued to want to do it, but I had to continue to let her know I thought it was too much to expect of her.

It was not fair, and I would wash the dishes if she could just help me fold the clothes. Some days we would go grocery shopping. Afterwards, we'd sit back on some days and laugh and talk for hours. We enjoyed making homemade yeast rolls together and she would assist me in that by giving me the ingredients. I noticed that Connie was not sure which ingredients to bring to the counter. I realized that it may have been time to give her some not-so-complicated tasks. Therefore, I would have her get out the pans we would be using or help me put away the ingredients after we used what we needed.

We would go visit family together and have a wonderful time. I organized a homeless feeding program, and I would take Connie with me. She was very helpful in doing things at that homeless shelter and she enjoyed doing that. As I mentioned in a previous chapter, Connie was able to help me plant a garden. Moreover, we could go out and even harvest the vegetables.

A typical day 5 years and 8 months later is not filled with joy and laughter.

I get up, start my day and on the days that Connie doesn't have a caregiver coming to the home, I must get myself bathed and dressed, have my breakfast and sit for a couple of hours before I go into Connie's room. I wake her up, walk her to the bathroom, get out clothes for her to wear for the day, bathe her, do her oral care, dress her, do her hair, take her to the TV room then go prepare her breakfast. I would cut the meals up into bite size pieces and made sure to give her medication. After Connie has finished her breakfast, some days it's as if she doesn't know how to feed herself. Yes, I do that too.

After breakfast, I sit with Connie and do a few coloring sheets. Sometimes it seems as though she doesn't know what to do with the coloring sheets. (I bought a few coloring books and I take out a page at a time for her to color to have something to give her to do.) We watch some TV together although she is not focused on the TV much anymore.

Connie doesn't do much long-distance walking anymore, but I do take her outside sometimes and walk on the street we live on. I prepare her lunch. I go through the same thing of cutting it into bite-sized pieces for her. I help in feeding her if she needs it. We don't do much between lunch and dinner other than sit on the porch and occasionally make a quick run to the grocery for one or two items. At the end of the day, I get Connie ready for bed and tuck her in for the night.

Connie sits now, and picks, twists and turns her clothing, like her pants legs. She pulls on strings, and she just doesn't really seem to be focused on anything except tampering with her clothes and her fingers. Connie twiddles her fingers and twists them around and twists it back. This is a kind of hand movement she does all the time but she's not doing anything constructive. I try to get her to do the color sheets and she doesn't even seemingly know how to hold the pencils or the crayons anymore to do them. It's extremely difficult, discouraging and depressing to watch.

Chapter 8

1) Five years after the diagnosis, what's one thing that has changed the most about you or your loved one?

CHAPTER 9: CONNIE WALKED AWAY

My biggest help and supporter with Connie has been my husband Yahya Talib. There was never any question in my mind as to if he would be right there by my side in the decision to make our home her home. I wasn't sure how much help he would be in caring for Connie.

Long before Connie was diagnosed with dementia, she used to help my husband as he was a vendor at the 500-mile race in Speedway for years. Connie and Yahya formed a close relationship during those times.

I was never one for sales, so I didn't go with them, but I recall the excitement as they shared the different stories of the day. It was very lucrative, and Connie loved that part of it because she enjoyed shopping at that time in her life.

When I talked to my husband about Connie coming to live with us he had also begun to see the decline in her health and he was all for her moving in with us.

After a while, with Connie living with us, my volunteering and social activities began to taper off as I needed to spend more time with Connie. Yahya would always encourage me to continue to do my volunteering as much as I wanted. It was fine for Connie to stay home with him as he was doing computer repairs; this was just one of the things he did after retiring.

One day I had an event to go to where I was the volunteer coordinator so I couldn't take Connie with me because I wouldn't be able to keep an eye on her. When I returned home, I prepared Connie's 6 o'clock meal. I went into the TV room to find that she wasn't in there, so I walked into her room to find she wasn't there either. Now I am yelling down into the basement to my husband, "Yahya, where is Connie?!".

He said, "She's upstairs." I looked in the backyard at this point. I am panicked, frantic. I'm screaming her name, "Connie! Connie!".

My husband rushes up the stairs. We look in the backyard. I said to him, "OK, she is not here."

"You take your vehicle, and you go south on our street. I'll take my vehicle and go north."

At first, I couldn't move. I barely got to my car because my legs were trembling so bad. I couldn't move at first. As I'm pulling out of my driveway, I receive a call from my husband.

"I got her.".

I'm yelling, "Where is she?! Where is she?!".

He said, "I'm at the corner of Kessler and 30th at the Walgreens."

When I made my way over to the Walgreens, which was just around the corner, not even a full block away, I was inconsolable. I saw an ambulance and I knocked on the ambulance door. I got no response, so I went inside the store. I was told, "We don't know what's going on out there."

I went back out and at this point, one of the paramedics stopped me and asked, "Are you looking for the lady that we have in the ambulance?"

I said, "I don't know. I'm looking for my husband and my sister, but I don't know who you have in the ambulance."

I looked through the window of the ambulance and saw my husband with my sister inside. The female paramedic began to console me and tell me my sister was OK. She had a card with a gentleman's name on it and she told me this gentleman brought her to Walgreens.

His story went like this:

> We found this lady walking, my wife and I. And I told my wife, "Something's not right! That lady doesn't have shoes or a jacket. It looks as though those are pajamas she has on."
>
> His wife told him, "Leave her alone. You're always messing with people; she's probably fine."
>
> He insisted, "No, I wanna turn back around and see if we can help her."

He stopped my sister and asked her, "Where are you going?".

She told him, "I'm going home to 3540 N. Capitol."

He knew there was no way this elderly lady could be walking that distance by herself with no shoes, wearing pajamas and no jacket and believing that everything was not OK.

So, he said, "Well, if it's OK can we take you?"

She told him, "Yes".

He took her back to the Walgreens at 30th and Kessler and called 911 to tell them he had a lady in his vehicle and their location and to send help.

The card had the man's phone number; he asked the paramedics to make sure to let him know how things turned out. She in turn gave me the card. I would like to share my husband's thoughts on the event.

According to him, as he turned the corner he saw red flashing lights at Walgreens, he said in his heart he knew it had to be Connie. He went over to Walgreens and asked the officer, "Is there a senior lady in there? Inside that ambulance? If so, I believe it may be my sister-in-law. She has dementia and she walked away from the house".

They allowed him to look inside the ambulance and found that it was Connie. He was able to get in and sit with Connie as she was extremely confused. Connie didn't know where she lived, who was her brother-in-law of thirty years, nor did she even know her own last name.

After getting Connie back home and situated, I called the number on the card. The gentleman that left the card was so kind and he told me, "I'm so glad your sister is OK. I knew in my heart something was wrong when I saw she didn't have any shoes. I took her back to Walgreens because it was a well-lit corner where I could have the police meet us versus saying we're at the corner of 30th and Coldspring Road. I was able to give Walgreens as a landmark and they came immediately".

I told him I wanted to thank him, and I wanted to give him some money as some type of reward for doing what he had done for my sister. I asked him if there was a way I could send money to his account. He continued to tell me, "No, just come and visit my church and bring your sister."

It was fine for me to go and visit the church and take Connie, but I still was very persistent in wanting to give him something. Finally, he gave me his information and I was able to send money to his account. I shared this information with my sisters and even one of my neighbors. We all sent money. It was a little joke between us about all the money we sent to him. He's probably riding around today looking for little lost old ladies.

That incident prompted deadbolts being put on all entry doors. My husband was so apologetic and continued to tell me, "I don't know how this could've happened."

Well, there's a first time for everything, she had never walked off before and thank God to this point, she has never again.

Chapter 9 - Reflection Questions

1) What is your worst fear about your loved one wandering off?

2) Why do you think they always want to go home (a place that is no longer theirs)?

CHAPTER 10: DEAD END

Well, you may imagine, this chapter is somewhat difficult for me because this chapter doesn't just tell my sister's story, it tells how dementia impacts the brain. I will also share with you, the reader, some insights into my observations of Connie's struggles and my own personal struggles as her sister/caregiver.

I titled this chapter 'DEAD END' for various reasons. Dementia is a terminal illness. It doesn't care how many degrees you hold, how many countries you've visited, or how much money is in your bank account. Not even what part of the world you're from. This build-up of plaque on the brain, narrowing or stenosis, finds and continues to invade until it has destroyed most of your faculties, irrespective of who you are.

I was so angry with dementia, and I wanted to know more about it. As is my habit, I began to research as much as I could about this disease. Something I discovered is one in ten people over 65 years of age has dementia according to a 2016 study reported in Medicine Net.

Someone shared some very powerful information regarding how the brain is affected by dementia and how dementia specifically affects language skills. I was astounded when I heard and saw the presentation that was given by Teepa Snow. Teepa Snow is an American dementia care specialist and occupational therapist.

She talked about the left side of the brain being the language side and the right side being the rhythm side where the automatic chitchat is found. The right side doesn't tend to forget the small talk, but it doesn't know how to articulate and/or make sense of words beyond that.

This helped me understand better how Connie related. When people would greet Connie at the house or doctor appointments, she was able to make small talk, but not much more than that. The small talk (chitchat) was instilled on the right side of the brain. Quickly though she would revert to the left side and not be able to make out words, complete sentences, or participate in conversations. Because portions of the brain have been destroyed, one no longer has the ability to recall or the ability to add new things to the memory bank. Personal care is greatly impacted as well.

Another reason this presentation was so extremely helpful to me was because I was never able to understand how it was that my sister was able to go visit with our siblings and they would tell me things like, “she had a pretty good conversation with me”. She seemed OK or “You know I didn’t see a lot going on with her in the way of not being able to have a conversation”. But now I understand it was because the conversation wasn’t lengthy that she was able to carry on with the side of the brain that stores those general conversations (chitchat). Such as, "Good morning, how are you?”

Connie replies, “I’m good”.

This is the extent of what my sister was able to do. When you got past those things and asked her other questions, she could not participate in the conversation much further than that. I didn’t understand how sometimes we would sit and talk, Connie would struggle to get words out and then someone would walk in the room and say,” Good morning, how are you, Connie?”

She would respond, “I’m good. How are you?”

I was just flabbergasted and couldn't understand. Viewing this presentation helped me understand what was actually going on with her and I hope the information shared by Teepa Snow will be as helpful to you as it was for me. I learned so much from this presenter. Her advice helped me to change my focus to what my sister can do, not the things she can't do. In the Resource Section of this book, you will find the link for this presenter, along with other valuable information.

Chapter 10 - Reflection Questions

1) What have you learned about dementia?

2) Do you have help and support with the care of your loved one?

CHAPTER 11: THE BIG PICTURE

I'm at a place now where I am beginning fully to accept the decision I made to move Connie in with me and the huge impact it has had on my life and family. I see the bigger picture now. I am possibly going to be forced to make some end-of-life decisions. That is if I should outlive her, I accepted the task of taking care of my sister. I believe I will be able to undertake the task of making sure things go the way she would wish for them to go at the time of her death. This opens another door of discomfort on several levels.

I will have to turn the end-of-life decisions over to my family to carry out the final arrangements for my sister. Not much has been mentioned to this point about our religious beliefs. Connie is a Christian and I am a Muslim. I would do things very differently at the time of the loved one's death as a Muslim; I would take the responsibility of washing my sister's body and shrouding her as Jesus was shrouded. If Connie were Muslim, she would be buried within three days of her death. I will take the responsibility of paying off all her debts whether business or personal. Connie has paid all her final arrangements with the funeral home and cemetery so that would make that part a bit less painful, but still very difficult.

You see, Connie has not gone to church on a regular basis since she has lived with me, but I still maintain that Connie is Christian. I did not and will not attempt to change anything as it relates to her Christianity in this process of laying her to rest, you might ask, what's the challenge? The problem is that although I would happily pay off her debts, on the other hand, I could not with a clear conscience plan a traditional Christian funeral nor give her a Muslim burial.

I wouldn't be able to allow her remains to sit for days while planning the wake, selecting songs, choosing a coffin, and all the other conventions that accompany Christian burials. As Muslims, we don't have coffins or huge headstones. Our funerals are simplistic. We don't even have flowers at our service and a customary Muslim funeral usually lasts no more than thirty minutes. However, making sure Connie has the proper services in line with her religious practice as a Christian will be my honor and duty.

Connie and I in the summer of 2021.

Chapter 11 - Reflection Questions

1) Whose life has your loved one's dementia affected?

2) How can you support each other? (If there are others.)

CHAPTER 12: THAT OTHER CHARACTER

Being as active as I was in my community, I realized I had to take Connie along with me on many occasions. Connie loved going and being a part of something. I mentioned in one of the earlier chapters that I had organized a feeding program at a homeless shelter. On the days my group went to the shelter Connie would be dressed and ready waiting on me. She loved going and being a part of that.

The way I looked at volunteering began to look and feel very different as Connie's dementia progressed. It used to be great having her along with me and even volunteering with me at different events and venues. Now having to assume the role of caregiver and watch her closely, I had to make sure she didn't go off somewhere or get confused with what she was doing.

The joy of volunteering and being very active in my community was no longer as joyful as it once was. I began to resent the fact that Connie couldn't be left alone at home, and she is less and less capable of being social and seemingly more confused at home as well as in public. From time to time, I still volunteer when I can leave Connie with family or a caregiver.

I think it is important to say here that you shouldn't lose yourself in your loved ones' illness. Try to maintain your sense of self and maintain as much of your normal routine as you possibly can. If you stop doing your normal routine this can cause resentment towards your loved one. I say to myself when I'm not able to participate in things because of Connie, maybe God was protecting me from some type of harm that may have been on the way to the location or even at the location. Thinking like that helps me to shift my perspective.

Chapter 12 - Reflection Questions

1) If not you then who? Answer how you choose.

CHAPTER 13: PARTICIPATING IN RESEARCH

I was contacted by one of the local hospitals, asking if I would be willing to enroll my sister in a research study they were conducting with people that have dementia. There are so many uncertainties about this disease that studies are being conducted every day to try to grasp as much information as possible for treatment plans, education, diagnoses, and anything else that can help medical professionals to be better equipped to manage the disease. It seemed the right thing to participate in this ongoing research. If something I shared about my sister's condition would improve another person's outcome later down the road, it would be my pleasure.

The research study was made up of two parts. One part consisted of social work the other nursing. The social worker was in her early 30's with a very calm and pleasant demeanor. However, she was more reserved and not as outgoing as the nurse, the nurse although around the same age as the social worker was more cheerful and extroverted.

Some of the study questions they asked:

*Has your loved one had any falls?

*Is your loved one still able to dress themselves?

*Can your loved one recall their full address?

*Can your loved one write their name?

*What is the furthest distance your loved one can walk?

There was even a short section included with questions pertaining to the caregiver.

When it came to discussing Connie's condition with the research team, I was very open because I was hoping to find answers through previous research and even help future families by answering the questions and giving insights about Connie's changes. I didn't feel like they were ever too personal and if they had been, I would've known how to handle it. That's just the type of person I am. Fortunately, it was very easy to talk and share with them about Connie's behaviors and the things that she was exhibiting so I didn't have any problem with doing that.

In all honesty, sometimes when they would come from the research team, I was not in the mood for sitting down to answer a lot of questions, but this is what I had agreed to. The research was conducted via phone and sometimes in person. They alternated months one month would be the social worker doing her assessment and checking in on how things were going with Connie. The nurse would come out or call the following month. They only came to the house a couple of times. Most of the study was conducted via telephone. I was given a binder with pages correlating with the questions that I would be asked. When I would receive the call from the nurse, she would have to turn to the section that pertained to her area. The nurse began to ask questions from that such as:

"What was Connie's weight?"

"Is Connie still walking and getting around on her own?"

"How was Connie's appetite?"

Each section would have the answer choices in different forms such as questions would sometimes be in the form of rating scale from 1 to 3 or options - like, dislike, satisfied, very satisfied, or dissatisfied.

The question sessions would last 30 to 45 minutes depending on which researcher was conducting the study that day. The nurse's calls always seemed to last a bit longer.

The social worker calls were based on how things were going with Connie as well as with me. These were some of the questions that were asked:

> "Over the past few weeks, have you been feeling down, depressed?"
>
> "What have you done for yourself to make yourself happy this week?"
>
> "What do you do for relaxation?"
>
> "Do you feel like you have adequate help with Connie?"

This research study lasted for 12 months. I participated in the research to help find some answers and or possible solutions for people with dementia. I realized that more people need to participate in these studies so that more information would be available about the changing dynamics of dementia.

Chapter 13 - Reflection Questions

1) Would you participate in a research study? Why or why not?

PART 2:

YOU'RE NOT ALONE

CHAPTER 14: MY MOTHER'S STORY: MEMORIES FROM SABOOR

Hello, my name is Saboor. Saboor is an Arabic name that means patience, which is what you need when caring for someone with Dementia or Alzheimer's disease. It's a progressive mental deterioration that can occur in middle or old age due to generalized degeneration of the brain. It is the most common cause of premature senility. Yes, patience is needed, as well as a healthy sense of humor.

I experienced this horrible disease with and through my mother; everyone called her Libby. I must begin by saying that although this disease is hard to witness, I can only imagine how it is to live through. For me, it was like going through different childhood diseases with my children. I was so glad I was there to at least attempt to make things better for her. Also, I must say, I was blessed because according to some of the caregivers I met in the support group provided by Central Indiana Council on Aging (CICOA) their situation had been a complete horror story. My mom, not so much, honestly, not at all. My mother was easy to care for: she was pleasant, happy and usually very content with the care I was providing, until one dark and rainy Sunday evening.

This evening started out like most Sunday evenings. My mother had gone to church and dinner with my older brother James, his wife Trena, and their son Jamar. Returning Mom home, Trena mentioned that Mom had been somewhat agitated during the service, and at dinner as well. They left, and I went to help Mom get undressed and into her night clothes. As she was undressing, she said, “I don’t care what anybody says, I’m getting out of here.”

I asked, “Are you okay?”

She said, “No! That darn James left me in the church basement all by myself!”

I asked, “When?”

Mom’s response, “Now, there is no one here but me!”

I said, “No Mom, you are here with me and Ashton (my son’s youngest child).”

Mom insisted she had been left alone in the church. At that moment, the phone, which was upstairs, rang. I tried to calm Mom down by reminding her she was at home, and in her housecoat, underskirt, and slippers, but she was not convinced with my answers. I informed her I was about to run upstairs to get the phone, but she was still complaining, so I ran upstairs. It was Trena.

(4:33 pm)

She was calling to check on Mom, again saying, "Mom had been sort of upset during church and dinner."

As I was explaining what Mom was saying, Ashton, who was two at the time, came upstairs and was trying to tell me something. I responded to him, "Wait one minute while I speak with Trena," and he went back downstairs.

(4:38 pm)

I talked to Trena for two more minutes. Ashton returns, again trying to tell me something. I told Trena, "I have to go to see what's up with Ashton."

(4:40 pm)

I went back downstairs, talking to Mom the whole time. I was explaining why she was not left in the basement and asked what she wanted to look at on TV. I suddenly became very aware that Mom was not responding, and I immediately panicked.

I looked in the bathroom, which was in her room, but she was not there.

I looked in the laundry room, which was connected to her bedroom but on the back porch. She was not there.

I searched the entirc ground level of our house.

SHE WAS NOT THERE!

I asked my grandson, "Did you see Granny?"

He slowly (as he does) looked up at me, taking time to stop his electric train, and said, "Yep" again starting his train.

I said, "Did she leave the house?"

Again, stopping his train, he said, "Yep" but held his stare as if to say, 'I tried to tell you twice, you ignored me, now let me play with my trains.'

Not saying another word, I grabbed Ashton, my purse, and my keys and headed out the door to find my mother. (4:42 pm)

It was just like in the movies. It was dark outside, and it had really begun to rain. I went up and down the street hoping to see an elderly lady in her housecoat and slippers, but no such luck. I knew where to check next.

My mother, as with most, if not all people with Alzheimer's Disease, have no or very limited short-term memory. However, their long-term memory is intact and functional. Mom was always speaking of going home. She was not speaking of where we currently lived, she spoke of the house she had lived in for over forty years. The house where she had raised nine children and cared for her elderly aunt and uncle, 1641 Cornell Avenue.

That was our next and only spot to check. SHE WAS NOT THERE.

(4:52 pm)

I realized this was totally out of control, I had to contact the police, but before that I **must tell my family**, after all, it would be too much to bear for them to see an amber alert on TV, searching for Marian E. Collins. I would have to leave the country and change my name.

(5:00 pm)

I systematically called each sibling, starting with the oldest, Sterling, he said he would be right over. I called my second oldest brother James. He and Trena were on their way. I called my oldest sister, Beverly, she instantly went into cussing, and praying mode, stating she also would be right over. The great thing about calling my sister Beverly is that I did not have to call the other five because she called the rest.

(5:10 pm)

I called the Indianapolis Police Department and explained the situation; they arrived in twelve minutes.

(5:22 pm)

There were two police units; they quickly asked me the most common of questions, “Do you have a picture of your mom?”

“What’s her name?”

“What is she wearing?”

“Anyone she may have tried to contact?”

He explained he had to check the entire house from the attic to the basement which they did with speed and determination, explaining that sometimes the loved one hid somewhere in the house, or might be too confused to get themselves back to the main part of the home. She was not there.

(5:30 pm)

The officer explained that one unit would stay with me, and the other would go out and search.

The family had started to arrive.

(5:35 pm)

As I was explaining to those who had arrived, I received a phone call, it was the officer who went on the search, they had found her! The officer explained that they had partnered with the Yellow Cab Company, and they use the police frequency for just this reason. It seems my mother had made her way to a local restaurant, soaking wet and in her night clothes, and asked them to call her a cab, which they did, and yes, she went home.

(5:45 pm)

The cab driver saw the house had been boarded up and no one lived there so he parked and waited, and finally he picked up the call of a missing elderly female in her night clothes.

(5:55 pm)

My mother was pulling up in a yellow cab, smiling, and waving like a beauty pageant queen, happy to see her children who she rarely saw anymore, and not even knowing she was wet, and she had been missing.

Of course, my family was trying to give me the business, but our oldest brother ran interference stating the obvious, none of you are even trying to care for Mom, she is doing the best she can.

The police officer informed us that this happens more than seven times a day, that is one reason they partnered with Yellow Cab to make sure our loved ones who do wander away from home, make it back safely.

We got Mom settled; everyone went home. I apologized to Ashton and promised him and myself that I would never ignore him again. I thanked Ashton for his part in the returning of my mother, and I would like to thank the Indianapolis Police Department, and the Yellow Cab company for returning my mother to us.

It appears my mom found my keys in my purse, opened the deadbolt, and stepped out into the night, looking for her home. She never did it again. Thank God.

CHAPTER 15: THE LESSON MY MOTHER TAUGHT ME: MEMORIES FROM SANDRA

Let me begin by saying my mother was born in 1918 and was raised with great morals and values; she was a virgin when she married my father, at the age of 33, in 1941. My mother graduated from Alcorn State University in Alcorn, Mississippi with a bachelor's degree in education; she then furthered her education earning her master's degree in education from Butler University in Indianapolis, Indiana.

I've worked in healthcare for 38 years starting in 1984 as a Certified Nursing Assistant then becoming a Qualified Medication Aide. I furthered my Education in 1987 attending Nursing School and earned my Nursing License in 1989.

In 1992 I started noticing changes in my mother's behavior. Mother would be very paranoid thinking family and neighbors were all against her. She told me that my husband was going up and down the street talking about her. Mother would be so upset, which upset me; she cried. I'd be on the phone balling people out because I'm thinking they're talking bad about her. People would say, "Sandra, I wouldn't dare say anything bad about your mother; I love her, she's my sister".

I confronted my husband. I yelled at my neighbors. I chastised all of those I thought were mistreating her; I even cussed out my oldest brother.

Two months later I came home after working my 12-hour night shift at the hospital. It had snowed all night; we had eight inches of snow on the ground. Thankfully, I made it home through the storm in my four-wheel drive truck. When I pulled up in the driveway, Mother was standing in the doorway waiting for me… or so I thought. I came in and she was standing in the door all dressed up with her makeup on, hair looking pretty, and I said, "You sure are dressed up this morning, what's the occasion?"

Mother responded, "I'm just waiting for my friends to come and pick me up; we're driving to Seattle, Washington today. They called me and told me to be ready at 8:00 o'clock this morning."

I said "Momma, it's a snowstorm out there, there's no way you and your friends are driving to Seattle Washington!"

Momma's response? 'I really don't want to go'.

"Okay, I'll call them and tell them you're not going". Momma agreed. I went to her phone and looked at her caller ID so I could call whoever it was that told her to be ready. There were NO CALLS on her caller ID. When I showed that to her, she got defensive and said, “I didn’t tell you they called, I told you they came over here yesterday and told me to be ready this morning!”

It was then that I knew we had a problem.

As time went on it became very clear to me my mother was suffering from Dementia. I then thought about all the people I accused of mistreating her, the multitude of people I balled out. I even thought of my great aunt in Mississippi that I called and confronted. She was 90 years old at the time. The only good thing about that call is that she was very hard of hearing. The entire time that I’m accusing her of mistreating my dear mother, she’s steady saying ‘hello hello hello’. So, I hung up because she couldn’t hear me, which I’m so grateful for because my mother was going through Stage One of Dementia which is Paranoia.

Mother’s condition was getting worse. She started becoming bladder incontinent and her bedroom started having a very strong smell of urine. I had my brother come take her out of the house so I could go through her room to try to figure this thing out. I couldn’t search her room while she was there because she always thought people were stealing from her. I did her laundry and just couldn’t find anything. In her dresser, I found panties that had been wet but were allowed to dry out without being laundered (multiple pairs). Because of her pride, she was too embarrassed to tell me she was wetting herself. Adult pull-ups then became a part of our household.

Time went on and her condition worsened. Being a nurse all these years, I really thought I was an expert on caring for Dementia patients. Not only did I care for them for many many years, we as healthcare workers must go to multiple Dementia In- Service Trainings throughout the year, 'State Mandated'. You must know how to deal with them, how to redirect them when they are having behaviors such as Sundowners, which means they get really confused at night. We learn what the saying means 'once an adult twice a child'. We know all of that and we can recite it in our sleep because we are the 'experts'.

My mother passed away peacefully in her sleep on January 28, 2004; she had been recently diagnosed with Leukemia. I didn't understand that. I told the doctors 'Cancer doesn't run in our family and no one in our family has ever had that diagnosis'. It wasn't until then that I learned my mother's brain had deteriorated so much that the part of the brain that produces bone marrow which produces red blood cells was no longer there. There was nothing there but a big hole! It was at that point her battle which she fought for 11 years was over.

For eleven years I watched Momma slowly die right in front of me. We healthcare workers have always called Dementia/Alzheimer 'The Long Goodbye'.

The Lesson My Mother Taught Me was no matter how much of an expert you think you are, you don't know the full impact an illness has on a family until it happens to you. I do for the first time clearly understand Dementia and I didn't learn it from a book or an in-service.

"I learned it from my mother."

Sandra Rogers

CHAPTER 16: MY LOVING MOTHER: MEMORIES FROM YAHYA

My name is Yahya Talib; Lana is my wife. I would like to share my experience with Dementia.

My mother was a very independent woman; she walked or rode the bus everywhere she went. This was after the divorce from my father. Mama did marry again, but that marriage ended in divorce as well.

What I remember about my mother is she would never ask anyone to do anything for her unless it was necessary. For 20 years I watched her walk down to 27th and Rader Street to catch the bus to go to work at the city-county building. My mother worked at the city-county building in housekeeping. That's where she started off, then she was promoted to supervisor. People who worked at the city-county building, in all departments, loved and respected my mother: Ella Frances Gill.

On weekends mama cooked meals. She would be in the kitchen cooking, listening to her blues and sipping her drink. As an adult, I would go to visit my mother and take her to the stores. But my mother also loved thrift stores, and one of her favorite stores was on Northwestern Avenue in

Indianapolis, Indiana. There were several stores there, but mama had her favorites.

I can recall during all the holidays, my mother would cook large meals and make sure that there was enough for my brother and I along with our families so that we could have food, fun and enjoy the time we spent with each other. I have to say I think Thanksgiving was Mama's favorite holiday.

She would smoke turkeys for herself, her family, lots of people who placed orders with her and people that worked with her at the city-county building. She enjoyed doing that. Mama would smoke her turkeys on a barrel-like grill that she had in her backyard, and she would use liquid smoke and Kingsford charcoal. She never used anything other than that; I can still taste it. I truly missed the times that we would get together and enjoy one another and Mama. I miss so much how Mama embraced all of us and brought us together.

After my mom was diagnosed with Alzheimer's everything changed. She had to stop cooking and doing so many other things. She was no longer able to be that independent woman that I'd always known her to be. As Mama's Alzheimer's disease progressed, I could still see bits and pieces of her, but she was never the same. Most of the time you would find Mama just sitting and staring into space. Sometimes she would watch TV.

If I played the blues for her, she would smile but nothing more than just a slight smile that let me know she was still in there. I was so extremely sad when Mama was diagnosed with Alzheimer's disease because it took away the vibrant, active woman that I knew her to be and if she wasn't watched closely, she would sometimes just walk off. My brother would have to go and find her and bring her back home.

When she was first diagnosed my wife and I wanted her to stay with us, but she didn't want to be away from her own home, so she stayed in her home and my younger brother took charge of her care. Mama would call my wife and I at three and four o'clock in the morning. Our phone would ring and when one of us would answer Mama wouldn't remember what she was calling for. This became a habit with her. We had to ask that the phone be moved away from Mama once she went to bed to keep her from reaching over and making phone calls. One day Mama was walking to the bus stop before her Alzheimer's disease progressed, and she was attacked by a Pitbull. This attack was very traumatic for

Mama. It took a very long time for the wounds to heal, and the psychological effects, I don't think they ever healed.

I think Mama suffered a great deal of emotional and psychological trauma that was added to her already altered state due to Alzheimer's disease. Mama was a lonely woman, but she still made the very best of everything. On top of Mama having Alzheimer's disease, she was also diagnosed with pancreatic cancer during a visit that my brother and I had taken her to.

We don't know how much pain Mama was in because she never voiced it. She never said anything about that matter. It wasn't long after the diagnosis that Mama was placed in a facility, and they started sedating her with morphine. I recall being very sad because she didn't talk at all once the Morphine was given. We were told they wanted to keep her comfortable. Mama seemed to stay in that semi-coma state for weeks until she finally passed away on my brother's birthday, April 12, 2006.

I just wanted to add there were times that were not so sad for me before Mama became ill. I would go visit Mama on some weekends and listen to blues with her as she drank her favorite drink, Remy Martin. She collected cans: pop and beer cans. She saved them up and cashed them in to have a lot of money that would help her when she was planning and preparing the meals. She would sell those cans to have that extra money so that her holidays would be exactly what she wanted them to be. I would pick her up on the weekends and we would drive behind nightclubs, and I would be the one to climb in the dumpsters and get out all the cans.

Mama was not a highly educated woman, but she was very intelligent. She knew how to save her money and be able to help if my brother or I needed anything. I miss seeing my mother's smiling face and her sparkling eyes. She had a very swift walk and I miss seeing that as well. Alzheimer's and dementia; it's truly no joke. They change the person that you love. Physically they're still there, but mentally and emotionally, they are changed. I have to say I hate dementia and Alzheimer's, what those diseases do, and what they did to my mother. I have a lot of love and respect for my younger brother because he stepped up and did most of the care for our mother and for that, I am truly grateful.

CHAPTER 17: MY LOVE FOR CONNIE: A FAMILY TRIBUTE

My name is Tiffany Linza, Aunt Connie's niece. Lana is my mother.

Well, there are many moments; however, her nurturing, loving spirit has always spoken to my soul. If I had to think of one moment it would have to be a special memory from my childhood. I remember Auntie coming to visit us in Briarwood apartments for some time. I couldn't wait to get home from school to talk to her and then later share our nightly ritual. Every evening, Aunt Connie and I would share a snack of celery and peanut butter in our large walk-in closet that we turned into our own little hideaway.

To know Aunt Connie is to know that she was the caregiver of our entire family.

My name is Gloria Lewis Vaughn; I am one of Connie's younger sisters.

My fondest memories of Connie are those where she epitomized Super Woman in my life. Connie, before her diagnosis, was always a Ready Warrior whenever I needed one. She was the Protector and Soldier, always ready to protect and vanquish any and everything that might present itself as a threat to me, real or imagined!

I felt cheated, relieved, sad, and somewhat angry; a myriad of emotions, when I learned of Connie's confirmed diagnosis.

- Cheated, because my Warrior was in fact, taking the long walk away from precious memories and her valued position as "Lifeguard On Duty" in my life.
- Relieved, because our family now had a name for all the unexplainable behaviors that Connie seemed to now exhibit.
- Sad, for the same reasons as I felt cheated; and then some.
- Angry, because there is no cure for this disease that seems to be quite comfortable and at ease visiting trauma upon our family.

So many simultaneous and mixed emotions.

Having prior experience in training and equipping caregivers of those with Dementia, I came to the table with foundational tools and information, as well as firsthand, experiential knowledge. However, what was reinforced for me is the fact that each case, each person, is unique. No two individuals take this journey the same. Therefore, everyone must be loved, cared for and encouraged, not as one has cared for another with the same diagnosis in days gone by, but according to the needs of the person at hand.

The destination is the same, yet the journey is vastly unique and different.

Any advice I would give should be taken with a grain of salt because as I previously stated, everyone is unique. However, having said that, it is always a good time to love, to practice patience, to make sure the caregiver is rested and reenergized to provide optimum care. You cannot pour from an empty or resentful cup.

During this journey, you will be faced with a vast array of emotions, tears, feelings of being overwhelmed and joy!

PLEASE TAKE FULL ADVANTAGE OF THE SITUATIONS AND DAYS THAT USHER IN THOSE SMILES. I SUGGEST YOU MAKE A TREASURE BOX AND JOT DOWN THOSE TIMES, ALONG WITH THE DATE...YOU WILL CHERISH THEM IN DAYS TO COME.

GOD BLESS YOU!

My name is Yahya Talib. I am the brother-in-law of Connie and Lana's husband.

I felt sorry for Connie when she was diagnosed with dementia because I didn't think she would be her feisty energetic self anymore.

Dementia changes a person's mentality and personality.

What I have learned with Connie living with us and me being able to see dementia firsthand daily is that you must be patient when caring for someone with dementia and you must take time for yourself.

My fondest memory is when she and my friend Jack went to the 500-mile race in Indianapolis, Indiana at the Speedway. My, what a pair! The three of us, and we always had such a great time every year.

We worked as vendors selling t-shirts and interacting with the crowd. Working at the Speedway required a lot of walking but gave access to lots of people. We saw people of every shape & size. Food trucks abounded and we ate our fill! We made great memories and lots of money as we talked and laughed the day away. Connie always looked forward to going each year and was still excited at the end of an exhausting day.

Connie at a family reunion White Party with three of our sisters and two nieces, 2023.

Connie at another family reunion White Party with a few siblings in 2019.

Connie dancing at the White Party.

Connie and Kenya dancing at the family reunion the next day, 2023.

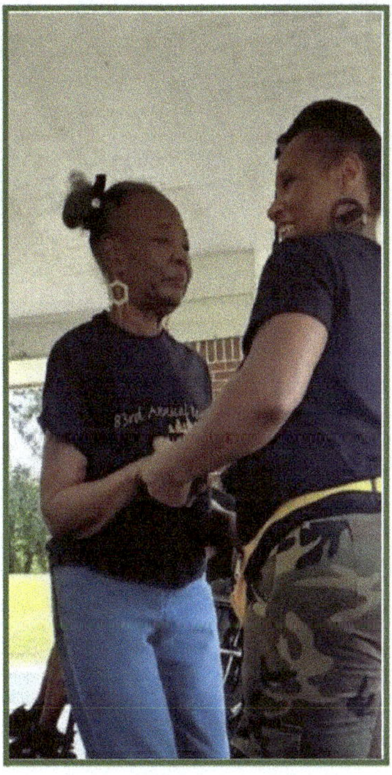

Connie and our youngest brother, James Lewis (Jimmy).

Connie, my husband, Yahya, and I.

Connie and a few of our siblings, summer 2022.

CHAPTER 18: NOTES FROM FRIENDS

My name is Mary Sullivan. I have known Lana Lewis-Talib for over 20 years. We have worked together on several projects throughout the years, and it has always been a joy. We are also close friends outside of work projects and it is an honor to call her my friend.

She is loyal, trustworthy, and very supportive. She is very talented, and her humanitarian efforts are many. Lana has strong community ties and is an active member of the Indianapolis community despite being the primary caregiver for her older sister who is facing some health challenges.

As I am writing this, I'm sure Lana is in the middle of juggling at least 10 projects with poise, ease and above all, a sense of humor. Since Lana has taken on the responsibility of caregiver, I've seen many of her activities have been altered to accommodate this role.

She brings her sister along to some of her volunteering activities such as the soup kitchen we used to do twice a month. Also, her sister accompanies her to Islamic holiday celebrations. Lana is a hands-on caretaker making sure her sister is clothed, fed, and engaged in activities that will keep her mind stimulated. She makes sure her sister is taken care of before she ventures out and to this end, she has made sure there is a well-trained professional to take care of her sister in her absence.

My name is Mu'mina and Lana has been my sister-friend longer than I can remember. If I had to guess, I'd say 24 years (based on the ages of my children). I moved to Indianapolis, IN in 1999 from Philadelphia, PA and I believe we met shortly thereafter. We sat in a meeting in the basement of Masjid Al Fajr, she was behind me, and I remember her saying, "How are you sister?".

I turned around and didn't recognize the face, though I smiled anyway. She introduced herself and mentioned a mutual friend from whom she'd heard about me (our friend has since died, RA (May Allah be pleased with her). I guess our friendship was inevitable since we 'ran in the same circles', but no one could've predicted how close we'd become! 'A straight shooter, hold no punches kinda gal' is how I describe Lana. If you wanted the truth (or not) she'd tell you! She is a talented cook, seamstress, author, etc., she is my friend.

As long as I've known her, she's always been a 'family person.' Whether her immediate or extended family: she was always there for them, to comfort, to love on, to hang out with. There were times when I asked her to go somewhere with me, she replied, "Oh, girl, I'm doing such and such with my sister", or "I'm going to my brother's".

There seems to have been a time when her mother lived with her, but I traveled quite a bit and may have left the country during that time. What I know for sure is, if her mother didn't live with her before she died, Lana's mother certainly stayed with Lana to receive comfort and care!

When Lana told me she wanted her sister Connie to live with her, I didn't blink! For the love she's always shown her family, that was certainly a 'Lana move.' I think I asked her how she would juggle all that's on her plate and especially the challenges her sister would bring, she retorted, "Well, she's my sister, I'll figure something out".

And praise the Lord, she did!

Her struggles with Connie seemed to have changed her life. Caring for someone you know only comes as a shock when you find that you 'used to know her/him.' Due to her disease, Connie's behavior was that of someone different, someone it took Lana time and prayers to accept!

Lana, as much as she could, provided Connie with a social life, took her to events which she attended, and always kept her sister looking nice. At one event, a woman sat across from me who I couldn't identify. Since no one introduced us, I asked Lana who she was. "That's Connie, my sister!" she exclaimed.

I'm sure wondering why I didn't recognize her. Lana had her looking so gorgeous (especially her hair, pulled back and in a bun)! In my defense, it wasn't so much that I didn't recognize her as much as it was that she was 'out of context!' Had we been at Lana's house (where I'd usually see her), I would've known!

As life goes, Lana told me that her sister is now in the latter stages of Dementia/Alzheimer's. In addition, Connie may not know how much she's loved and cared for by her sister, but she *is* loved and cared for.

May Allahu T'ala (The Most High) grant you paradise for your selfless work! Ameen.

My name is Lillian Abdur-Rahman. I met Lana Lewis-Talib more than 20 years ago, perhaps closer to 25 years ago at a gathering in her home. After meeting Lana on several occasions, I discovered many things about her. The one fact I found most impressive is "she is a real worker"! If you need to get something done, get Lana on your team (that's what I did).

When thinking about Lana I think of her in the three different roles as witnessed during our time together. These roles include family, friends, and community. In each of these roles she displays compassion when needed but shares her perspective and appears authentic in her relations with each.

Lana and family:

I found family to be very important to Lana. Over the years I've observed her relationship with siblings, her children, and grandchildren. After observing Lana interacting with family on numerous occasions, it was evident that family is number one on her list.

I've visited her home many times, spent time with Lana while she cared for her mom, as a daughter and caregiver. I observed firsthand the gentle loving care provided by Lana and her siblings while caring for their mom. As Lana now provides care for her sister, Connie, it demonstrates yet again how sacred family is. I know part of this is due to her Deen (religion), but also based on the family values instilled from childhood, Allah knows best.

Lana - Friendship and workmanship:

I consider Lana a true friend. While residing in Indianapolis for many years, I personally have solicited Lana for assistance on numerous projects. Some projects were one-time events, other projects included short term, long term, and even annual events. Projects varied in nature, some were fun, simple, and relaxing, such as gardening.

Other projects related to health education in the Muslim community and/or the general community. Lana was always willing to partner with different organizations, without hesitation. I've enjoyed working with Lana over the years due to her work ethics. Knowing she will follow through on whatever she agrees upon provides a sense of peace. If she committed to taking on a specific assignment, you could count on the job getting done.

As related to friendship, I found an excellent walking partner. Walking in the evening after work, on weekends, early mornings in the mall, or in the neighborhood it didn't matter. It was always great to have her as a walking partner. Of course, during these walks we'd often discuss projects, or simply enjoy each other's company. I admit many of the topics mentioned above were prior to Lana taking on the responsibilities of caring for her sister on a full-time basis.

Lana and the Community: My perspective looking from a distance.

Over the many years of friendship with Lana, she's always been a busy person. I've known her to always have a few projects going on in the background at any given time. When it comes to the Janazah (funeral /burial), regardless of what was on her plate, Lana seemed compelled to work with those experiencing the loss of a loved one. Lana is frequently called upon when there's the death of a female in the community.

She's called on for her knowledge related to the washing and shrouding of the Muslim female in preparation for the Janazah of the deceased. Lana has participated in providing this service for many years, both in hands-on experience, and educational workshops. In addition, she has worked in preparing and making available pre-packaged Janazah kits for years as well. Sharing this information with younger generations is crucial, with both Muslim and non-Muslim communities. I pray she continues with this important work, along with teaching others this practice.

Working with Lana for more than two decades was and is always enjoyable. She's good company, has good conversation, and the opportunity to catch up on many topics. Although I'm no longer in the city, I know I can still count on her when needed during important times. Lana can also count on me whenever a need occurs.

I applaud Lana for writing this book and pray Allah will provide her with what she needs while she continues to provide needed care for her sister, Connie.

EPILOGUE

I have worked on this book for over 3 years.

I would jot down memories from time to time, then I would put it all away because life wouldn't allow me time to focus on it.

I would get anxious when I saw people around me publishing their books no matter what the title or the subject matter was. I felt like my book should be finished because I started before them, however, I would pull it back out and begin writing again until it faded out once more.

One day I realized this story is telling itself daily and I'm not able to rush an ending to this story. This story is living itself out right in front of me.

Connie now qualifies for in-home doctor's appointments. She had her first nurse practitioner in-home visit, and it went well. This visit consisted of a lot of information gathering and the normal physical assessment: vital signs, weight and walking distance in the house. Connie seems to light up when someone comes to see her. The appointment was the highlight of her day. She is scheduled to be seen each month.

Moving forward, I think the in-home visits are going to work better for Connie and me. We don't have to worry about getting out in unfavorable weather conditions or having to sit in a doctor's office with other patients that may have viruses, colds or other illnesses that Connie could potentially catch. I think to this point she has been very fortunate not to have had any major illness that would cause her to be hospitalized.

This has been the most challenging yet rewarding life experience. While Connie's mind continues to progressively decline, our only hope is to make her comfortable and love her through this process. She is teaching us patience, how to be good caregivers and self-introspection, advocating for ourselves and prioritizing self-care. Connie is a fighter and she's struggling to maintain some sense of who she used to be. We may never see that person again, but we have loving memories and hope she has felt the love and support given to her.

To my immediate family you have my permission if I come this way. Please write my story if it will help someone.

Lana Lewis-Talib

RESOURCES

Common types of Dementia

Parkinson Dementia

Mixed Dementia

Frontotemporal Dementia

Vascular Dementia

Lewy Body Dementia

Alzheimer's Dementia

**Alzheimer's is the most common type of Dementia*

Articles:

A 19 Year Old is Youngest Ever to be Diagnosed with Alzheimers
https://www.psychiatrist.com/news/a-19-year-old-is-youngest-ever-to-be-diagnosed-with-alzheimers/#:~:text=A%20case%20study%20reported%20on,early%20onset%20of%20the%20disease.

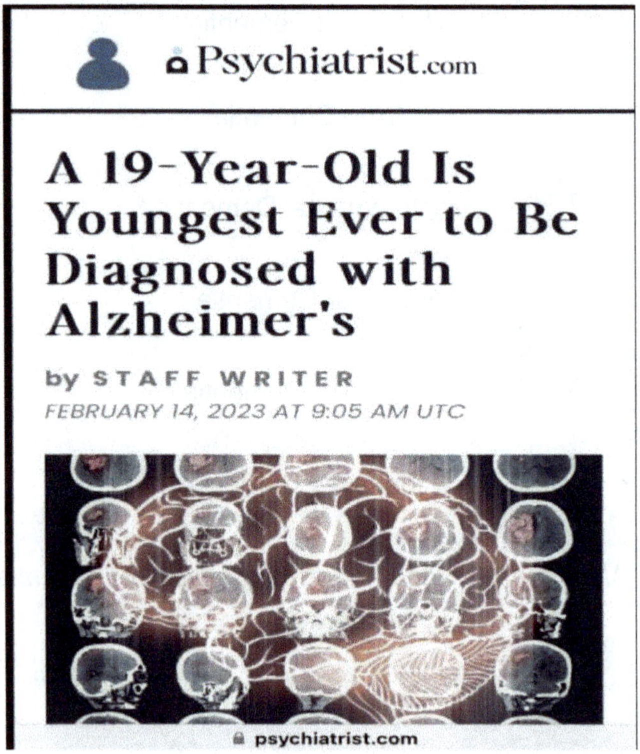

Psychiatrist.com

A 19-Year-Old Is Youngest Ever to Be Diagnosed with Alzheimer's

by STAFF WRITER
FEBRUARY 14, 2023 AT 9:05 AM UTC

psychiatrist.com

Helpful Information:

Signs That It's Time to Call Hospice -

Here are a few standard signs and symptoms that indicate your dementia patient or loved one is ready for hospice care.

- If your patient is unable to move about and ambulate without assistance.
- If your patient is unable to dress and undress without assistance.
- If your patient is unable to bathe or clean themselves properly.
- The person with dementia is suffering more hospitalizations and doctor's visits than usual.
- They start to suffer from incontinence and frequently soil themselves.
- They have trouble eating, drinking, and speaking on their own.

If your dementia patient or loved one is suffering from these afflictions regularly, it may be time to contact hospice.

5 Key Messages

- •Dementia is not a normal part of aging.
- •Dementia is caused by diseases of the brain.
- •Dementia is not just about having memory problems.
- •It is possible to have a good quality of life with dementia.
- •There's more to a person than dementia.

https://www.alzheimers.org.uk/about-dementia/five-things-you-should-know-about-dementia

Links:

Alzheimer's Association - https://www.alz.org/

Caregiver Resources:

- National Alliance for Caregiving, www.caregiving.org
- Today's Caregiver, www.caregiver.com
- Family Caregiver Alliance, www.caregiver.org
- Caregiver Action Network, caregiveraction.org
- National Caregivers Library, www.caregiverslibrary.org
- The Well Spouse Foundation, www.wellspouse.org
- Positive Approaches to Care (Teepa Snow) https://teepasnow.com/

NIA Alzheimer's and related Dementias Education and Referral (ADEAR) Center -
www.nia.nih.gov/alzheimers
800-438-4380
adear@nia.nih.gov
CareAware – www.careawarejourney.org

Legal Services:

- Indianapolis Bar Assn (Lawyer Referral), www.indybar.org, 317- 269- 2000
- Legal Line (free consult by Indianapolis Bar Assn) – 2nd Tues ONLY, 6-8 PM, 317-269-2000
- Neighborhood Christian Legal Clinic, www.nclegalclinic.org
- Senior Law Project (specialize in Elder Law; must meet financial eligibility), www.indianalegalservices.org/node/legal-services-senior-law-project, 317- 631- 9424

Senior Wellness:

- Health for Seniors, www.usa.gov/health
- National Center on Elder Abuse, ncea.acl.gov
- National Institute on Aging, www.nia.nih.gov/health
- Nursing Home Abuse, www.nursinghomeabuse.org

Alzheimers.gov - www.alzheimers.gov

- Explore the Alzheimers.gov website for more information and resources on Alzheimer's and related dementias from across the federal government.

Alzheimer's Association - www.alz.org

800-272-3900
866-403-3073 (TTY)
info@alz.org

Alzheimer's Foundation of America -
www.alzfdn.org

866-232-8484
info@alzfdn.org

ACKNOWLEDGMENTS

This book would not have been possible without the support of my dear sister/friend Leanna Abdelmaged.

She worked tirelessly with me to bring this book to the hands of you, the reader.

Leanna looked at what I presented to her and began to ask me question after question about each chapter. As I started to answer her questions, I realized each chapter was increasing. She checked and changed sentence structure, punctuation and even some spelling. Leanna gave of her time even in the face of her own physical and emotional challenges.

Leanna was very professional with me and at the same time personable. My sister/friend knew how much I wanted to share this story with you. As a friend she stepped up to help yet we had to maintain a sense of professionalism and not to cross any lines that would hinder the process. I am and will forever be grateful to my sister/friend Leanna Abdelmaged. My sister, friend, beta reader, editor, and supporter.

I am grateful to Rebecca Kendall for sharing her words of encouragement as she willingly did edits on some of the earlier chapters of this book and volunteered to be a beta reader.

I thank Mumina Blackman for her role in editing and beta reading. Listening to, laughing with, and keeping me on track with my timelines.

I am forever grateful to Sandra Rogers for sharing her mother with me as well as her story to be placed in my book.

When I asked Saboor Robinson about sharing any part of her experience with dementia/ Alzheimer to go in my book, she did not hesitate. She asked about my deadline, and she met it with ease; I so appreciate her.

Cover Design by Damone Means.

A huge thank you to Shar'ron Mason for all of her support.

And finally, my gratitude to Linky Ugeh is great. She took on the role of primary editor and offered invaluable guidance on the formatting requirements.

URGENT PLEA!

Thank You for Reading My Book!

I really appreciate all your feedback and
I love hearing what you have to say.

I need your input to make the next version of this book and my future books better.

Please take two minutes now to leave a helpful review on
Amazon, Goodreads, or your other social media platforms letting me know your thoughts on the book.

Thanks so much!

Contact the Author:
Lana Lewis - Talib
authorlanat@yahoo.com

www.ingramcontent.com/pod-product-compliance
Lightning Source LLC
Chambersburg PA
CBHW071439090426
42737CB00011B/1721
* 9 7 9 8 2 1 8 3 1 1 5 9 9 *